Read
Responsibly™

Other **UNSHELVED** collections by Bill Barnes & Gene Ambaum:

Unshelved

What Would Dewey Do?

Library Mascot Cage Match

Book Club

Read Responsibly™

an UNSHELVED® collection
by Bill Barnes and Gene Ambaum

...but not too responsibly.

OVERDUE MEDIA

Seattle

FOREWORD

I'm a cartoonist.

Which, for those unfamiliar with the profession, basically means I didn't date much in high school. Or college. But it also means that my professional life is centered around laughing. I'm *paid* to find things to laugh at…to find funny things in life. Which is good, because I can tell you without hesitation that the book you're holding in your hands is hilarious.

I know this, because I'm also a *jealous* cartoonist.

I'm jealous of how funny *Unshelved* is on a daily basis. Bill Barnes and Gene Ambaum have, with their hugely popular comic strip, stumbled on a kernel of truth that hundreds of TV sitcoms have missed: that the library is a funny, funny place. It's a mashup of people, places, ideas, triumphs, failures, introverts, extroverts, meanness, kindness, and unexpected humor. It's not just a repository of humanity's knowledge, it's a repository for how weird we truly are. And *Unshelved* captures that wonderful weirdness with utter brilliance.

Which, in the end, makes me a *laughing* cartoonist.

Or rather, a laughing reader. I can't be jealous of Bill and Gene…how can I? They've made me laugh before I can work up a fit of jealousy. Like you, all I can do is enjoy the ridiculous (but scarily, all-too-real) daily antics of the Mallville Library staff. These *Unshelved* characters – these *people* – make my life a little easier, a little happier, and a lot more joy-filled.

So read on! I can guarantee you'll be laughing out loud by page 10.

Trust me: I'm a professional.

Dave Kellett creates the daily comic strip *Sheldon*, which can be read daily at <u>www.sheldoncomics.com</u> and in three book collections: *Pure Ducky Goodness*; *The Good, The Bad & The Pugly*; and *62% More Awesome*.

WHAT IF EVERYONE IN MALLVILLE READ THE SAME BOOK?

WHAT IF WE JUST ATE THE SAME FLAVOR ICE CREAM?

I'M SERIOUS. WE'LL HOST BOOK DISCUSSION GROUPS AND ... BOOK DISCUSSION GROUPS.

REMEMBER A BRIEF HISTORY OF TIME? EVERYONE BOUGHT IT, BUT TRY TALKING PHYSICS WITH THOSE PEOPLE.

WHATEVER. YOU'RE IN CHARGE.

"WHAT IF EVERYONE SAID THEY READ THE SAME BOOK?"

COULD WE BRIBE PEOPLE INTO READING THE SAME BOOK?

THAT'S A LOT OF PIZZA.

THERE'S NO BUDGET FOR INCENTIVES. READING IS ITS OWN REWARD.

THEN IT WILL HAVE TO BE NAUGHTY.

"WHAT IF EVERYONE READ THE SAME SMUT?"

OUR GRANT WON'T COVER THAT.

THAT'S A LOT OF BOOKS.

I'M TRYING TO PICK ONE THAT EVERYONE IN TOWN WILL READ.

WON'T YOU HAVE TO BUY, LIKE, A ZILLION COPIES?

YEAH. THERE'S A GRANT.

THEN IT'S EASY. JUST ASK THE PUBLISHERS FOR A KICKBACK AND GO WITH THE HIGHEST BIDDER.

DON'T THEY TEACH YOU ANYTHING IN LIBRARY SCHOOL?

I COULDN'T FIND A BOOK THAT EVERYONE IN MALLVILLE WOULD READ.

THEN I THOUGHT, LOWER THE BAR!

"WHAT IF EVERYBODY WATCHED THE SAME EPISODE OF CHEERS?"

I OBJECT.

NO, YOU'RE RIGHT. TOO DATED.

...THEN SHE PICKED UP THE BOOK AND

...EXCUSE ME.

HOW DOES YOUR STORY END?

YOU'LL HAVE TO READ MY BLOG. I HATE REPEATING MYSELF.

I SAID "SECTS" NOT "SEX"!

SORRY, MY MISTAKE.

TAP TAP TAP

ARE YOU LOOKING FOR THE BOOK?

NO, I'M BLOGGING. HOW WOULD YOU DESCRIBE YOURSELF -- "MALNOURISHED" OR "SKIN AND BONES"?

I NOTICED YOU'VE BEEN DOING A LOT OF BLOGGING.

GOTTA FEED THE BEAST. THE BEAST IS ALWAYS HUNGRY.

TAP TAP TAP.

TAP TAP TAP.

YOU'RE BLOGGING THIS CONVERSATION, AREN'T YOU?

MAYBE. WHAT ARE YOU GOING TO SAY NEXT?

TAP TAP TAP.

COLLEEN, YOU'RE SPENDING TOO MUCH TIME BLOGGING INSTEAD OF DOING YOUR JOB.

I'M FACILITATING A FRICTION-FREE INFORMATION ECONOMY. ISN'T THAT MY JOB?

GOT YOU RIGHT IN YOUR LITTLE BLEEDING LIBRARIAN HEART, DIDN'T SHE?

WHY AREN'T YOU FACILITATING ANYTHING?

YOU'RE REARRANGING THE BOOKS?

I'M FIGHTING COMPLACENCY.

ALSO WIDELY KNOWN AS "EASE OF USE".

STUDIES SHOW THAT PRODUCTIVITY WILL INCREASE BY 37.2%!

I WENT LOOKING FOR SMALL ENGINE REPAIR, BUT I FOUND MYSELF IN TEEN ROMANCE. AM I LOSING MY MIND?

YOU WOULDN'T BE ALONE.

PUT SCI-FI NEXT TO THE POTTED PLANT!

YOU'RE NOT UPSET BY ALL THESE CHANGES?

DON'T BE SILLY. CHANGE IS GOOD FOR THE SOUL!

THEN YOU WON'T MIND THAT I MOVED ALL YOUR STUFFED ANIMALS.

LOOK, MEL'S EXPERIENCING CHANGE.

I DIDN'T KNOW TAMARA KNEW WORDS LIKE THAT.

IT'S KINDA SEXY.

READ

MY OFFICE IS... EMPTY.

WE WANTED TO MAKE SURE YOU WERE ON YOUR TOES.

MANAGER

HOW AM I SUPPOSED TO GET ANY WORK DONE?

GOOD QUESTION. I'D ANSWER IT, BUT I NEED TO FIGURE OUT OUR NEW SHELVING ARRANGEMENT.

WHAT DID YOU DO WITH BEATRICE?

YOUR FICUS?

I THINK I SAW IT IN THE ASTRONOMY SECTION.

THAT WAS HER STAPLE REMOVER.

IT'S HARD TO KEEP THINGS STRAIGHT THESE DAYS.

EAD

OKAY, YOUR OFFICE IS BACK TO NORMAL.

AS IS THE LIBRARY.

I HOPE YOU REALIZE HOW MUCH YOU'RE STUNTING YOUR PROFESSIONAL DEVELOPMENT BY MAKING IT SO EASY TO FIND THINGS.

WHERE'S CAR REPAIR?

THE SAME PLACE YOU COULDN'T FIND IT LAST WEEK.

IS THAT A FACT?

CLOSE ENOUGH.

REMEMBER TO RECORD THAT TRANSACTION. IT'S SURVEY WEEK.

BUREAUCRATIC NONSENSE. IT'S NOT LIKE OUR JOBS DEPEND ON IT.

MEL? YOU'RE WORRYING ME HERE.

SOMEBODY ASK ME A QUESTION!

THERE HAVE BEEN RUMORS.

IT'S SURVEY WEEK, SO WE WANT A LOT OF QUESTIONS, RIGHT?

WE'RE JUST GATHERING STATISTICS ABOUT OUR CUSTOMERS.

BUT IT WOULDN'T HURT IF OUR CUSTOMERS WERE WILDLY INQUISITIVE.

LET'S JUST SAY CURIOSITY NEVER KILLED THE LIBRARY CAT.

LOOK WHAT I FOUND IN FOREIGN PERIODICALS!

READ

IT'S "80'S FLASHBACK WEEK" ON THE RADIO.

JENNY I GOT YOUR NUMBER I NEED TO MAKE YOU MINE

SO I ADDED ANOTHER LINE TO THE REFERENCE DESK.

JENNY DON'T CHANGE YOUR NUMBER

WHAT DOES THIS HAVE TO DO WITH SURVEY WEEK?

EIGHT SIX SEVEN FIVE THREE-OH NINE

R-RING!

NO, JENNY'S NOT HERE.

DO YOU HAVE ANOTHER QUESTION?

WHAT HAPPENED?

IS EVERYTHING OKAY?

ARE WE IN DANGER?

ENTER AT YOUR OWN RISK

SLOW DOWN, I NEED TO COUNT YOUR QUESTIONS FOR SURVEY WEEK.

EMERGENCY ZONE

POLICE LINE - DO NOT CROSS

EXTREME HAZARD

This space intentionally left blank.

DID YOU HEAR? A LIBRARIAN FROM MALLVILLE HAS A BOOK TALK THAT'S GUARANTEED TO MAKE PEOPLE FAINT.

THAT'S TERRIBLE!

I'D USE IT ON THE LITTLE SNOT WITH THE SUPERBALL.

UH UH. MISTER "MY TAX DOLLARS PAY YOUR SALARY" ALL THE WAY.

I FORBID YOU TO GIVE YOUR BOOK TALK.

THAT SMACKS OF CENSORSHIP. AND YOU KNOW WHAT THAT MEANS.

RING RING RING RING !!!

POPULARITY.

YES, I'M THE ONE WITH THE FORBIDDEN BOOK TALK.

SORRY, I DON'T DO CHILDREN'S PARTIES.

THAT'S A LOT OF READING MATTER, EVEN FOR A LIBRARIAN.

MY LAST BOOK TALK MADE SOMEONE FAINT.

HMMM, TANTALIZING.

I WANT TO WIDEN MY REPERTOIRE. WHAT ELSE CAN A BOOK TALK ELICIT? TEARS? RAGE?

WELL, JANE AUSTEN MAKES ME QUEASY.

THAT'S A START.

I DON'T APPROVE OF YOUR EXPERIMENTS.

I NOW HAVE BOOK TALKS THAT GUARANTEE CRAMPS, NAUSEA, AND MILD ECZEMA!

THAT DOESN'T SOUND VERY USEFUL.

OH, AND ONE THAT MAKES YOU SPEAK URDU.

THAT'S IMPOSSIBLE!

WAISE MAINE DELHI ME APNE MASHUK SE SEEKHA HAI.

REAL LIBRARIANS USE CARD CATALOGS, NOT COMPUTERS.

REAL LIBRARIANS USE REFERENCE BOOKS, NOT THE INTERNET.

WHAT'S WITH ALL THE SWEET TALK?

REAL LIBRARIANS—

FOR THE LAST TIME, I'M NOT GOING OUT WITH YOU!

I THINK IT WAS BLUE.

YOU THINK? YOU SAID IT WAS YOUR CELL PHONE.

LOST & FOUND

A DARK COLOR.

AND YOU DON'T KNOW THE BRAND? OR THE MODEL?

CAN'T I WORK WITH SOMEONE ELSE?

NO. I HAD THE HONOR OF LOSING THE COIN TOSS.

SO WHAT YOU REALLY WANT IS TO RIFLE THROUGH OUR LOST AND FOUND FOR VALUABLES.

AH, YOU UNDERSTAND!

NO.

"NO" AS IN "NO I DON'T UNDERSTAND"?

"NO" AS IN "IT'S MY JOB TO SAY 'NO' TO YOU."

BUT I WAS SO CLOSE!

THIS PHONE HAS BEEN IN OUR LOST AND FOUND FOR FOUR MONTHS. SAY I GIVE IT TO YOU.

YOU'D DO THAT?

LOST AND FOU

LET'S SAY I DO. THEN WHAT WOULD YOU HAVE?

I'D HAVE A PHONE?

BUT YOU'D NEED TO PAY FOR A SERVICE PLAN, A CHARGER...

IS THERE ANY CASH IN THERE?

MERV HAS AN IDEA.

HOLD ON.

SHOOT.

THE LOST AND FOUND IS FULL OF VALUABLE ITEMS THAT ARE NEVER CLAIMED.

TRUE.

WHY NOT AUCTION THEM ON EBAY?

GOOD IDEA. LET ME REFER YOU TO OUR ECOMMERCE SPECIALIST.

BID BID BID!

ACTUALLY WE'RE SELLING.

WE MADE $273 ON OUR LOST AND FOUND AUCTION.

THAT'S GOOD!

BUT IT TOOK COLLEEN AND ME THREE DAYS TO LIST EVERYTHING AND SHIP IT OUT.

THAT'S BAD.

BUT I WAS THE HIGH BIDDER ON THIS PEN THAT MAKES FART NOISES.

THAT'S...

WHERE DID YOU FIND MY PEN?

ONE OF OUR COMMUNITIES HAS REQUESTED LIBRARY SERVICE.

I'M NOT DRESSING UP.

I THINK I CAN ACCOMMODATE THAT.

MALLVILLE NUDIST COLONY AND FROZEN BANANA STAND

WE WERE EXPECTING A BOOKMOBILE.

I'VE GOT THIS DOLLY.

AH, YOU REJECT INTERNAL COMBUSTION LIKE WE REJECT CLOTHING, SHEDDING THE YOKE OF CONVENTION PLACED AROUND YOUR NECK BY A SOCIETY OUT OF TOUCH WITH ITS ANIMAL NATURE.

WE JUST CAN'T AFFORD ONE.

CONFIDENTIALLY? THAT'S WHY I STOPPED WEARING PANTS.

LET NO ONE EVER CHALLENGE MY COMMITMENT TO MY PROFESSION.

DEWEY.

NED.

YOU KNOW THIS WEIRDO?

CHANGING ROOM

NO, IN THE CASE OF REVENGE OF THE SITH I REALLY THINK THE NOVELIZATION WAS BETTER THAN THE MOVIE.

AND I DON'T USUALLY SAY THAT.

YOU'RE HANDLING THE WHOLE "NUDE THING" VERY WELL!

COMPARED TO MY NORMAL DAY THIS IS A WALK IN THE PARK.

DO YOU HAVE THIS IN A CLOTHES-FREE EDITION?

WHICH ISN'T TO SAY THERE AREN'T SIMILARITIES.

THERE'S SOMEONE AT THE GATE FOR YOU. CLAIMS HE'S YOUR ASSISTANT.

I WANT TO SEE LIVE NUDE GIRLS!

THANK YOU FOR YOUR PRESENTATION TO THE SENIOR CITIZENS!

CATCH YOU LATER.

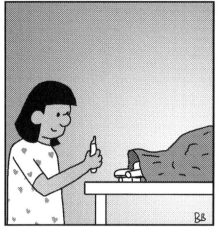

WHY DOES EVERY CHILD IN MALLVILLE EXPECT A COMPUTER AS A SUMMER READING PRIZE?

THERE WAS A MISPRINT.

READ AND GET A COMPUTER NO EXCEPTIONS!

I'LL GO TELL THEM.

I DON'T THINK YOU SHOULD DO THAT.

DO WHAT? MEET A PROBLEM HEAD-ON WITH OPEN HONESTY?

EVER SEEN WHAT HUNGRY WOLVES DO TO A LAMB?

I CAN'T LET THAT HAPPEN TO EWE!

READ

ON BEHALF OF THE LIBRARY I APOLOGIZE. THERE'S BEEN A MISTAKE!

NOT EVERYONE WINS THE GRAND PRIZE. THERE'S ONLY ONE COMPUTER --

I CAN TAKE CARE OF MYSELF!

I KNOW. WE'RE PROTECTING THE MOB.

READ

BUT FOLKS, READING IS ITS OWN REWARD!

YOU'RE SAYING WE OWE EVERYONE A COMPUTER?

YOU BROKE THE LAW OF UNINTENDED CONSEQUENCES.

I'M OKAY WITH GIVING AWAY ALL OUR COMPUTERS!

WHAT'S THE STATUS OF PLAN B?

THE FALSE CEILING ISN'T STRONG ENOUGH TO HOLD ALL OF US.

READ

YOU HAVE A PROBLEM. AND I AM A PROBLEM SOLVER.

WE DON'T NEED YOUR HELP.

THE LIBRARY ACCIDENTALLY PROMISED A COMPUTER TO EVERY KID IN TOWN.

DEFINE "COMPUTER."

WHAT DO YOU MEAN BY THAT?

HMMM.

BUT THIS IS MADE OF CARDBOARD!

I'M SORRY I --

LETTER OF THE LAW, KID.

NEXT!

BB

LESSON ONE: PIÑA COLADAS. AND IF THAT DOESN'T WORK, MORE PIÑA COLADAS.

YOU'RE GETTING DATING ADVICE FROM RANDY?

NOW LET'S TALK MEDALLIONS. THEY CAN NEVER BE TOO BIG. OR TOO SHINY.

HE HAS A WAY WITH WOMEN.

YEAH, A WAY TO MAKE THEM FILE RESTRAINING ORDERS.

IF SHE SLAPS YOU, IT MEANS YOU'VE HIT A NERVE. MOVE IN FOR THE KILL!

I GOT YOU SOME FLOWERS.

OH BUDDY, YOU'RE SO SWEET! ONE DAY YOU'LL MAKE SOME NICE GIRL VERY HAPPY.

THAT'S GOOD, RIGHT?

NURSE, PLEASE NOTE THE TIME OF DEATH.

I'M HERE TO PICK UP YOUR FUZZY FRIEND.

I THINK BUDDY'S TOO HEARTBROKEN TO...

LET'S GO!

ARE YOU SURE YOU'RE UP TO THIS?

YOU KNOW WHAT THEY SAY: "UNLUCKY IN LOVE, LUCKY IN COCKFIGHTING."

HOW'S MY LITTLE PRUSSIAN RED?

SKWAWK!

THE LIFE-SIZED CHEWBACCA I REQUESTED?

NO, IT'S OUR VERY FIRST PUBLIC ART!

THE COUNTY TEAMED UP WITH LOCAL BUSINESS LEADERS TO GIFT US THIS MASTERPIECE!

SO THERE WAS A FIGHT OVER WHO HAD TO TAKE THIS THING AND WE LOST.

WE WEREN'T EVEN AT THE TABLE.

HAVE YOU LOOKED INSIDE?

I'M WORKING UP THE COURAGE.

SO OUR PUBLIC ART IS...?

A STATUE OF ISAIAH MALL, CITY FOUNDER AND FIRST MAN TO PUT A LOGO ON A SHOPPING BAG.

IT'S ATTRACTIVE AND PERFECTLY APPROPRIATE.

I WONDER WHAT'S WRONG WITH IT?

THERE DOESN'T HAVE TO BE ...

IS IT MELTING?

WHAT'S HAPPENING TO MR. MALL?

THEY COULDN'T AFFORD TO HAVE HIM CARVED FROM MARBLE.

WHATEVER IT IS SEEMS TO HAVE A LOW MELTING POINT.

IT CAME FROM MALLVILLE

MAYBE WE CAN SAY HE LIKED CANDLES.

LADIES, GENTLEMEN, AND MEMBERS OF OUR VALUED TRANSGENDERED COMMUNITY, I PRESENT TO YOU... ISAIAH MALL, FOUNDER OF MALLVILLE!

ISAIAH MALL
CITY FOUNDER AND FIRST MAN TO PUT A LOGO ON A SHOPPING BAG

WHY IS THERE A BAG OVER HIS HEAD?

AFTER HIS NOSE FELL OFF, IT MADE THE MOST SENSE.

EXCUSE ME, I JUST REMEMBERED I LEFT SOME CHOCOLATE IN MY CAR.

I'M EXPLAINING WHAT HAPPENED TO OUR BRAND-NEW STATUE.

I THINK YOU DESERVE A HAND FOR THE WAY YOU DEALT WITH IT.

VEIO

IS THIS ALL THAT'S LEFT?

THE CHESS CLUB'S HAULING AWAY THE TORSO NOW.

TELL THEM WE RETURNED THE ART TO THE COMMUNITY THAT PAID FOR IT.

YOU SCARE ME SOMETIMES.

I HEAR YOU'VE BEEN TEACHING TAMARA TO SAY "NO".

SHE'S JUST TOO NICE FOR HER OWN GOOD.

HEY TAMARA, WANT TO CATCH A MOVIE TONIGHT?

NO.

YOU COULDN'T HAVE WAITED UNTIL AFTER I ASKED HER OUT?

WE'RE STILL CALIBRATING.

ARE YOU SURE THE COPIER IS OUT OF TONER?

PRETTY SURE

DID YOU REMEMBER TO PRESS 'COPY'?

YES.

IS THE DARKNESS CONTROL ON ZERO?

NO.

DID YOU PHOTOCOPY A BLANK PAGE?

NO.

WHY DON'T YOU JUST CHECK THE TONER CARTRIDGE?

I CHECKED IT THIS MORNING. YOU'RE RIGHT. IT'S OUT.

THEN WHY THE INQUISITION?

FORCE OF HABIT.

BB

CAN'T YOU PUT NEW TONER IN THE COPIER?

WE'RE OUT. BUT I'VE PUT IN A SERVICE CALL.

WHEN WILL IT BE WORKING AGAIN?

TOMORROW.

HOW DOES THAT HELP ME NOW?

YOU GET THE SATISFACTION OF KNOWING YOU'VE SET A MIGHTY BUREAUCRACY IN MOTION.

YOU FILLED THESE OUT WRONG.

BB

THE COPIER ISN'T WORKING. IT JUST PRINTS BLANK PAGES.

LET'S EXAMINE THAT WORD "WORKING."

I SHOW UP AT THE LIBRARY FIVE DAYS A WEEK. I TAKE ORDERS. I GO THROUGH THE MOTIONS, MAKING THE RIGHT SOUNDS AND APPEARING TO FOLLOW PROPER PROCEDURES. IF AT THE END OF THE DAY I DON'T HAPPEN TO HAVE ANYTHING TO SHOW FOR IT, CAN IT REALLY BE SAID THAT I WASN'T "WORKING"?

YES.

FORTUNATELY THE UNION DISAGREES.

LIBRARY TIP # 31: IF YOU DON'T WANT IT, THE LIBRARY DOESN'T WANT IT

I'M AFRAID THAT, BECAUSE OF COMMON ALLERGIES, WE HAVE A "NO DOGS" POLICY.

MY DOG'S NOT WITH ME.

NO, BUT YOUR SWEATER IS COVERED WITH HIS HAIR.

DO I HAVE TO BE NAKED TO USE THE LIBRARY?

DON'T BE RIDICULOUS.

I'D LIKE TO COMPLAIN ABOUT THE TEMPERATURE. AGAIN.

YOU'RE THROWING ME OUT?

YEP. DON'T COME BACK FOR A MONTH.

WHERE DO I FILE MY APPEAL?

RIGHT HERE.

WHATEVER HAPPENED TO THE BALANCE OF POWERS?

LOOKS LIKE IT'S TILTED IN MY FAVOR, DOESN'T IT?

I JUST GOT OFF THE PHONE.

YOU THREW OUT A KID THIS MORNING?

HE WAS LOUD AND OBNOXIOUS.

I'VE BEEN ASKED TO REVIEW THE CASE.

THEN HE TOLD ME, AND I QUOTE, "██████"

IF YOU DON'T UNDERSTAND WHAT THAT MEANS I CAN DRAW YOU A DIAGRAM.

I HAVE MORE NEWS ON THAT BOY YOU BANNED.

DID HE GO ON A MULTI-STATE CRIME SPREE?

NO, HE FILED AN APPEAL BEFORE THE LIBRARY BOARD.

THE HEARING IS SET FOR TONIGHT.

THEN I'D LIKE TO REQUEST THE AFTERNOON OFF TO PREP.

WHY, SO YOU CAN SEE A BARGAIN MATINEE OF SNAKES ON A PLANE?

LIKE I SAID, PREP.

I'M SORRY, WE HAVE A "NO CELL PHONES" POLICY.

I'M TALKING QUIETLY. YOU LET PEOPLE TALK QUIETLY, RIGHT?

YES, BUT...

WHY DON'T YOU HAVE A POLICY AGAINST EXCESSIVE VOLUME? WOULDN'T THAT MAKE MORE SENSE?

SHELDON, GET THAT DUCK OUT OF HERE!

PROFESSIONAL REASONS.

THERE'S BEEN A COMPLAINT ABOUT THIS MAGAZINE.

WE CAN'T GET RID OF SLOWRIDER!

THAT MODEL'S SKIN-TIGHT CLOTHING ENCOURAGES PHYSICAL FITNESS.

THE ARTICLES INSPIRE AN INTEREST IN MECHANICAL APTITUDE.

THOSE PAINT JOBS ARE A WORK OF ART.

WE NEED TO...

...DEMONSTRATE IT SERVES THE COMMUNITY.

GIVE ME 24 HOURS.

WHAT HAVE YOU GOT FOR ME?

OUR NEW PROGRAM ON VEHICLE CUSTOMIZATION AND AUGMENTATION.

WHAT'S THAT SOUND?

THE BASS LINE TO TOTAL ECLIPSE OF THE HEART? IT MUST BE OUR INSTRUCTOR!

MEL, MY OLD AUTO SHOP TEACHER, MR. VALENZUELA.

TURN AROUND, BRIGHT EYES!

EVERY NOW AND THEN I FALL APART.

THIS ISN'T A LIBRARY PROGRAM.

IT'S JUST A BUNCH OF KIDS READING PARTS CATALOGS.

IT'S ALREADY INSPIRED A SLEW OF REFERENCE QUESTIONS...

WHERE CAN I FIND BRAILLE DASHBOARD INSTRUMENTS?

HOW MANY GOLDFISH CAN LIVE INSIDE AN ODOMETER HOUSING?

MAN, THIS IS GOING TO BE SICK.

THAT MEANS IT'S GOOD.

INDEED, I AM ALREADY NAUSEOUS WITH ANTICIPATION.

Common Mistakes

- Too specific
  - *Will work for canned peas*

Common Mistakes

- Too specific
  - *Will work for canned peas*

- Too threatening
  - *Give me money or else*

I'D SAY OUR NEW "NO CELL PHONES" POLICY IS A BIG SUCCESS!

RING! RRING! HELLO? RING! YES? HELLO? YES, I'M FREE. RINGADINGDING! ZOOP! ZOOP! SURE, I CAN TALK! RING! AUNT CLEMMIE! HI! RING! No. RING

DEFINE "SUCCESS." NO BLOODSHED. OW, MY ARM!

LIBRARY TIP #32: DON'T FEED THE LIBRARIANS

HOMEMADE BROWNIES? I WANTED TO THANK YOU FOR ALL YOUR HARD -- STAFF SNACK BREAK! I ALSO NEED A LITTLE HELP WITH -- THAMAKARK

YEA VERILY, IS NO ONE MAN ENOUGH TO FACE ME IN THE LISTS? TAKE CARE OF THIS.

THAT'S NOT WHAT I MEANT. AIM FOR THE YELLOW PAGES.

WORLD ATLAS

I'M AFRAID WE DON'T ALLOW... SHE'S A SERVICE DOG.

OPENS HER MAIL. KEEPS HER WALLET WARM.

DOGS ARE COMPANIONS WHO CAN PROVIDE MANY LEVELS OF SERVICE!

SCARES OFF PURSE SNATCHERS. CHOOSES HER LIPSTICK.

DO YOU HAVE ANY THAT BARK AT RUDE PEOPLE?

HOW ABOUT WARN YOU WHEN SOMEONE'S WEARING TOO MUCH PERFUME?

NO, YOU MAY NOT HAVE YOUR OWN SERVICE DOG.

CAN HE MAKE COFFEE?

GRAPHIC NOVELS HAVE NO PLACE IN THE LIBRARY!

THEY'RE READ AND ENJOYED BY MEMBERS OF OUR COMMUNITY.

WELL I DON'T ENJOY THEM.

I'M WILLING TO BET YOU DON'T ENJOY MUCH.

I WANT THEM GONE!

I WANT YOU GONE.

AND, FRANKLY, I WISH I WEREN'T HERE EITHER. BUT LET'S TRY TO FIND SOME COMMON GROUND.

PEOPLE WHO READ GRAPHIC NOVELS SHOULD BE ASHAMED!

OKAY, HOW ABOUT THIS:

WHENEVER ANYONE GOES NEAR THE GRAPHIC NOVELS A GIANT FOGHORN WILL SOUND, A BANK OF SPOTLIGHTS WILL TRAIN UPON THEM, AND A LOUDSPEAKER WILL SHOUT THEIR NAME, WHICH WILL ALSO BE POSTED ON OUR WEBSITE.

PERFECT!

DARN IT, MY MOTION DETECTOR BUDGET FOR THIS YEAR IS TOTALLY SHOT.

I WANT YOU TO PUT THE GRAPHIC NOVELS WHERE NO ONE CAN FIND THEM.

I'M AFRAID WE CAN'T DO THAT.

THEN I'M TAKING THEM ALL. AND I'M NOT BRINGING THEM BACK.

I HOPE YOU HAVE A LOT OF MONEY IN THE BANK. THE FINES WILL BE ASTRONOMICAL.

THEN I'LL RETURN THEM AND IMMEDIATELY CHECK THEM OUT AGAIN.

PERFECT. THE HIGH CIRCULATION NUMBERS YOU'LL GENERATE WILL LET ME BUY EVEN MORE REPULSIVE TITLES.

GRAPHIC NOVELS

SCRAM! THESE BOOKS ARE NO GOOD FOR YOUNG PEOPLE.

IN THAT CASE I WANT TWO!

LOOK! A CHILD ENJOYING COMICS!

YES, DESOLATION JONES—A DRUG ADDICT EX-SPY TRACKS DOWN PORNOGRAPHY STARRING ADOLF HITLER.

TELL ME YOU'RE KIDDING.

DON'T WORRY. FOR ALL WE KNOW IT'S THE SORT OF THING HIS MOTHER WANTS HIM TO READ ABOUT.

MA'AM!

I'M JUST GLAD IT'S NOT MY JOB TO PARENT ANYBODY.

NO, HE DOESN'T SUSPECT A THING.

TAP TAP TAP

YOU WORRY TOO MUCH.

YES, HE WOULD KILL YOU, BUT HE WON'T, BECAUSE HE DOESN'T SUSPECT A THING!

HOLD ON.

TAP TAP TAP

ARE YOU RECORDING THIS?

THE TECHNICAL TERM IS "TRANSCRIBING," AND YES, I AM.

WELCOME TO THE OVERHEARD IN THE LIBRARY BLOG.

TAP TAP TAP

YOU CANNOT TRANSCRIBE PEOPLE'S CONVERSATIONS IN THE LIBRARY!

THERE'S NO REASONABLE EXPECTATION OF PRIVACY IN A PUBLIC SPACE.

WELL WE HAVE RULES. NOT TO MENTION A PROFESSIONAL CODE OF ETHICS.

IF YOU DON'T STOP I'LL... YOU'RE TAKING DOWN EVERY WORD, AREN'T YOU?

PLEASE, CONTINUE WITH YOUR SPECIFIC THREATS. YOU'VE GOT FIRE.

TAP TAP TAP

HOW'S YOUR OVERHEARD IN THE LIBRARY BLOG?

ADVERTISERS WON'T LEAVE ME ALONE.

AREN'T YOU BOTHERED BY PROFITING OFF THE VIOLATION OF PRIVACY?

HELLO, I'D LIKE TO BUY SOME COMMERCIAL REAL ESTATE FOR MY INTERNET STARTUP.

I GUESS YOU'VE REACHED YOUR PEACE WITH IT.

NOPE, PRICE IS NO OBJECT.

WHAT'S GOING ON?

I THINK THEY CALL IT "SILENCE."

IT'S... GOLDEN.

I MEAN, I'VE HEARD STORIES OF QUIET LIBRARIES, BUT I THOUGHT IT WAS A MYTH.

CAN I WRITE DOWN MY QUESTION? I DON'T WANT THAT YOUNG MAN TO TRANSCRIBE IT.

CAN YOU ALSO STOP BABIES FROM CRYING?

I WANT YOU TO STOP BLOGGING WHAT YOU HEAR IN THE LIBRARY. NOBODY'S TALKING AND THE SILENCE IS DISORIENTING.

OKAY, JUST GIVE ME FIFTY THOUSAND DOLLARS.

YOU KNOW I CAN'T AFFORD THAT.

A THOUSAND.

A HUNDRED.

TWENTY?

I TAKE IT YOUR STARTUP FAILED?

NO TALKING, NO BLOG. IT WAS A SELF-DEFEATING PHENOMENON.

HOW MUCH CASH DID YOU BURN THROUGH?

WANT TO BUY A STENO MACHINE?

LIBRARY TIP #33: DON'T MAKE YOURSELF AT HOME

YOU CAN'T WATCH THAT HERE.

AND HE MISSES THE FIELD GOAL!

COUCH POTATOES

THAT'S EXACTLY WHAT MY WIFE SAID.

I LOVE NATIONAL NOVEL WRITING MONTH. IT'S A GREAT WAY FOR WRITERS TO TRY OUT LONG FORM BY PUMPING OUT SHEER VOLUME.

SURE, THE QUALITY WON'T BE VERY HIGH, BUT IT'S A LEARNING EXPERIENCE.

IS THAT YOUR FIRST CHAPTER.

CONTRACT FROM MY PUBLISHER.

CONTRACT?

DOES THIS ADVANCE SEEM TOO HIGH?

I'M DONE.

BUT THE MONTH ISN'T OVER YET.

IT'S JUST FIFTY THOUSAND WORDS.

YEAH, BUT THEY HAVE TO BE IN A CERTAIN ORDER.

LIKE ANYONE CARES. BESIDES, I'VE GOT TWO SEQUELS AND A SCREENPLAY TO WRITE.

YOU WON'T REGRET PICKING ME AS YOUR AGENT.

LET'S TALK LICENSING.

THE ACCOUNTANT IS COMING!

WHAT ARE YOU SO WORRIED ABOUT?

SHE'S RESPONSIBLE FOR BALANCING OUR BOOKS.

WHAT BOOKS? ALL PURCHASING IS DONE CENTRALLY.

WE COLLECT OVERDUE FINES.

IN TEN CENT INCREMENTS. OUR CASH BOX GIVES NEW MEANING TO THE WORD "PETTY."

GOOD MORNING!

FROM YOUR UNREASONABLY CHEERFUL AIR, I INFER YOU HAVE SOMETHING TO HIDE.

FROM THE COLD SWEAT RUNNING DOWN MY MANAGER'S SPINE, I INFER YOU'RE OUR ACCOUNTANT.

I'M ON TO YOU.

IF YOU WANT TO SCARE ME YOU'LL NEED TO COME UP WITH A LINE I HAVEN'T HEARD BEFORE.

THE ACCOUNTANT WILL INTERROGATE YOU NEXT.

YOUR LIBRARY IS THIRTY CENTS SHORT LAST QUARTER.

THIRTY CENTS? HAVE YOU DUSTED FOR FINGERPRINTS?

THIS IS SERIOUS.

I'M JUST GLAD CSI: MALLVILLE IS ON THE SCENE.

I NEED TO RECONCILE THIS FINANCIAL DISCREPENCY.

HERE YOU GO.

SO YOU CONFESS!

I'M JUST HELPING YOU BALANCE THE BOOKS.

YOU CAN'T DO THAT!

BACK OFF. I'VE GOT A WHOLE POCKET FULL OF CANADIAN NICKELS.

DING-DONG, THE ACCOUNTANT IS GONE.

HOW'D YOU GET RID OF HER?

CREATIVE PROBLEM AVOIDANCE.

THAT MEANS I SHOULDN'T ASK, RIGHT?

I'VE TOLD YOU BEFORE — IF YOU'D JUST LET ME DO WHAT I'M GOOD AT, YOUR LIFE WOULD BE EASIER.

I CAN'T DECIDE IF THAT'S AN OFFER OR A THREAT.

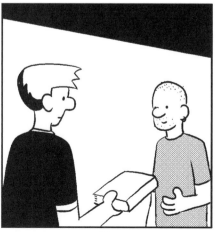

SOMETIMES I FEEL LIKE WE LIVE IN AN AGE OF EXTREMES.

WOULD HALF OF MY ORGANIC GLUTEN-FREE LOCALLY-GROWN VEGAN SANDWICH MAKE YOU FEEL BETTER?

LOOKS LIKE THE PROBLEM TOOK CARE OF ITSELF.
BB

I SAW IT FIRST.
I GRABBED IT FIRST.
SHE WOULDN'T LET IT GO.
HIS PHYSICAL STRENGTH AVAILED HIM NOT.
I DEMAND YOU LET ME CHECK THIS BOOK OUT.
NO, IT'S MINE!
AS FAR AS THE LIBRARY IS CONCERNED YOU'VE BOTH BOUGHT HALF OF IT.
BB

THIS IS ABSURD! YOU CAN'T CHARGE US FOR THIS!
YOU CAN'T FINE US FOR A BOOK WE NEVER CHECKED OUT!
DID YOU JUST AGREE WITH ME?
DID YOU USE THE FIRST-PERSON PLURAL?
DID THEY PAY?
NO, BUT THEY LEFT, SO IT'S STILL A VICTORY.
BB

TOFURKEY'S READY!
ALAS POOR TOM, I KNEW HIM WELL.
I THINK THAT'S A VEGETABLE.
LEGUME.
MOM, CAN I PLAY GAMES WITH DEWEY?
WHY DON'T YOU PUT THAT DOWN AND HAVE SOME POTATOES?
SO YOU CAN SEIZE THE GOOD CONTROLLER? NEVER.
READ
BB

YOU FOUND IT! THAT WASN'T SO HARD, WAS IT?

BLEEP!

HA! I REPLICATED THE BARCODE FOR THE BOOK I LOST, AFFIXED IT TO THE COVER, FABRICATED A CUSTOM R.F.I.D. CHIP, AND FAKED YOUR "MALLVILLE PUBLIC LIBRARY" STAMPS.

YOU... CLONED OUR BOOK?

COST ME A SMALL FORTUNE. BUT AT LEAST I DIDN'T PAY YOU.

WHAT DAY OF THE WEEK IS THE SECOND THURSDAY OF THE MONTH?

IT'S GOING TO BE ONE OF THOSE DAYS.

I'LL GET THE GEAR.

ONE OF WHAT DAYS?

IF YOU HAVE TO ASK YOU'RE PART OF THE PROBLEM.

THE BOOK I WANTED WAS SHELVED IN THE CHILDREN'S AREA.

OKAY.

BUT I'M NOT A CHILD!

OKAY.

ARE YOU SAYING I'M CHILDISH?

NOT YET, BUT YOU'RE OFF TO A GOOD START.

...BUT SHE WAS PUTTING THE CARDS INTO THE CARD CATALOG UPSIDE-DOWN!!

THOSE WERE THE GOOD OLD DAYS.

WHEN, THE BIBLIOLITHIC ERA?

BB

ALWAYS GIVE PEOPLE WHAT THEY WANT.

LAST WEEK A GUY ASKED ME FOR MY LUNCH.

OBVIOUSLY I'M JUST REFERRING TO LIBRARY MATERIALS.

HIS GIRLFRIEND WANTED TO MAKE A PAIR OF SLACKS OUT OF *CATCHER IN THE RYE.*

SHE WAS PULLING YOUR LEG.

YOU SHOULD HAVE SEEN HER *SILAS MARNER* HOODIE.

NEXT, A TRUST EXERCISE. PLEASE FIND A PARTNER.

DEWEY.

COFFEE?

BEATRICE.

DYING FOR IT.

WHERE ARE YOU TWO GOING?

TRUST US.

IS THE TRAINING OVER?

IT IS FOR ME.

WHAT DID YOU LEARN?

WHEN THE STUDENT IS READY, THE TEACHER WILL COME.

WHAT DID YOU REALLY LEARN?

SOMETIMES PUBLIC SERVICE BEATS AN ALL-DAY TRAINING.

WHAT'S THE TENSILE STRENGTH OF THIS BOARD BOOK?

REFERENCE DESK.

YOU'RE OUT OF WHAT?

WHY DID YOU TAKE THAT TISSUE FROM MY OFFICE?

I'M ANSWERING AN URGENT REFERENCE QUESTION.

WE'RE HERE FOR THE FREE BOOK.

WOW, LOOKS LIKE SOMEONE'S BEEN DOING A LOT OF READING.

IS YOUR DAUGHTER HERE? OR DO YOU WANT TO PICK OUT THE BOOK FOR HER?

SHE'S RIGHT HERE.

YOU KNOW THAT'S A DOG, RIGHT?

OF COURSE!

IN THIS BUILDING YOU NEVER KNOW.

I'M AFRAID PETS DON'T QUALIFY FOR READING PRIZES.

SHOW ME WHERE IT SAYS THAT IN THE RULES!

WELL I CAN'T, BUT

EVERYONE SAYS I SHOULD READ TO MY CHILD!

IF SHE WERE HUMAN YOU'D LET HER ENTER.

EXACTLY MY POINT.

THIS IS DISCRIMINATION AGAINST SINGLE PEOPLE!

ACTUALLY IT'S DISCRIMINATION AGAINST PETS.

WHICH IS STILL LEGAL.

MY DOG LOVES BOOKS!

HOW DO YOU KNOW?

LOOK WHAT SHE DID TO MAURICE SENDAK!

LOOK WHAT WE'RE CHARGING YOU FOR THAT!

I'M SORRY, BUT YOUR DOG ISN'T ALLOWED IN THE BUILDING.

BUT SHE--

IT'S THE RULE. YOU HAVE TO LEAVE.

-- LOVES THE LIBRARY!

THAT'S WHAT THE LAST GUY SAID. WE'RE STILL TRYING TO GET THE CARPET CLEANED.

YOU LOOK SURPRISED.

I CAN'T BELIEVE YOU STOOD UP TO THAT DOG LOVER!

WHY?

BECAUSE SHE HAD A POINT. HER TAXES PAY FOR KIDS' READING PRIZES. EXCEPT SHE'S DECIDED NOT TO HAVE KIDS, SO SHE'S NOT ALLOWED TO BENEFIT.

BUT I WASN'T GOING TO CAVE.

THAT'S A MANAGER'S JOB.

MA'AM! WAIT! THE LIBRARY WANTS TO MAKE YOU HAPPY!

WILL YOU FORGIVE MY FINES?

I DOUBT IT.

THIS BOOK YOU RECOMMENDED **STINKS**!

REALLY? I ENJOYED IT.

NO, IT LITERALLY STINKS.

YOU WANT A WHIFF?

NOT UNLESS THAT'S A FLOWER YOU'RE HOLDING.

I JUST DON'T UNDERSTAND IT.

ME NEITHER. NOT SINCE THE TURNTABLE.

WHY DO YOUNG PEOPLE CHOOSE TO ISOLATE THEMSELVES?

HOW DO THEY FIT ALL THAT MUSIC INTO THOSE LITTLE **THINGS**?

MAYBE IT'S A CRY FOR HELP.

MAYBE MUSIC USED TO BE BIGGER.

THAT GUY HAD NO IDEA I ALMOST LANDED ON HIM!

AND SO, THANKS TO MP3, A MAJOR LAWSUIT WAS AVOIDED.

I'M WARMING TO THIS NEW TECHNOLOGY.

Gene Ambaum:
Evolution of an Artist

by Bill Barnes

Drawing a daily comic strip is a great blessing, no question, but every so often I need a break. So Gene and I came to an arrangement. Every year on my birthday Gene would draw the strip. Once a year isn't that much of a break, it turns out, but it has proven to be an entertaining (and educational) tradition.

Educational because changing places yields huge dividends of empathy. Usually I'm the one with "final cut," making last-minute changes to a piece of dialog because it wouldn't fit in the panel, because the character's expressions makes it redundant, or just because it feels right. So it's good for Gene to make those choices and let me see how it feels. And it feels horrible. That man is a saint, I tell you true.

Entertaining because, as the one who usually puts off drawing the strip until the deadline or beyond, it's satisfying to see to what extremes Gene will go to procrastinate putting ink on paper.

But the most satisfying thing is getting to see him grow and mature as an artist. At one strip a year it's like the jerkiest stop-motion movie ever, but I can definitely see him improving. And here, for the first time in one place, you can too. So next January 13th please cheer him on. And, of course, wish me (and Dewey) a very happy birthday.

P.S. On his birthday we do jokes about toilets.

2003: Already Gene is showing great artistic economy, omitting unecessary lines such as "necks".

2004: My personal favorite of the birthday strips. That Sleestack totally rocks.

2005: The clip-art Ned completes the surreality of this strip which no-one, including Gene and I, understood.

2006: When I injured my back Dewey did too. Gene helped out by whining endlessly about how hard this was to draw.

A WINDSTORM IN MALLVILLE? I DON'T BELIEVE IT.

BAM!

WHOOSH!

OKAY, I BELIEVE IT.

WOW! IT BLEW ME RIGHT TO THE BOOK I WANTED!

THE COMPUTERS ARE WRECKED!

OUR FILES ARE A JUMBLE!

THE BOOKS ARE SCATTERED ACROSS THE LIBRARY!

BUT ON THE PLUS SIDE, OUR WORKSPACES HAVE NEVER BEEN SO UNCLUTTERED!

I DIDN'T KNOW MY DESK WAS THAT COLOR!

THE WIND KNOCKED OUT MY POWER.

I'M SORRY.

I'M LOOKING FOR A THICK BOOK.

TO READ BY CANDLELIGHT?

THE STORES ARE OUT OF FIREWOOD.

LET ME SHOW YOU TO OUR CLASSICS.

OUR COMPUTERS STILL AREN'T WORKING, SO WE NEED TO TAKE DOWN LIBRARY CARD NUMBERS AND THE BARCODES FROM ALL THE ITEMS TO BE CHECKED OUT.

AND WHEN THEY START WORKING AGAIN, WHO IS GOING TO ENTER ALL THE DATA I WILL BE PAINSTAKINGLY RECORDING?

YOU.

JUST BRING 'EM BACK IN A FEW WEEKS.

I'M SURPRISED TO SEE YOU HERE.

I'M A MANAGER. I HAVE LOTS OF PAPERWORK.

I UNDERSTAND YOUR JOB.

THEN WHAT'S SO SURPRISING ABOUT SEEING ME AT MY DESK?

GUESS.

I'VE DECIDED THE WAY TO DEAL WITH PROBLEM BEHAVIOR IS TO PUT MYSELF IN THE MIDDLE OF IT.

NOW I'LL BE ABLE TO KEEP AN EYE ON THINGS.

I'LL KNOW WHO'S RESPONSIBLE.

AND I'LL FILL OUT THE CORRECT FORMS!

I'D LIKE TO SEE THEM MISBEHAVE NOW!

I'D LIKE TO SEE YOU GET SOME WORK DONE NOW.

I DON'T KNOW HOW ANYONE DOES THEIR JOB AROUND HERE!

WELL WE DON'T USUALLY PUT OUR DESKS IN THE MIDDLE OF THE LIBRARY.

IT'S TIME FOR YOUR SHIFT. I'M COMMANDEERING YOUR DESK.

OH NO YOU DON'T. THIS WAS YOUR CRAZY IDEA.

HOW AM I SUPPOSED TO DO MY JOB?

I DOUBT THE PUBLIC WILL HAMPER YOUR ABILITY TO LOAF.

HOW DOES DEWEY USE THIS COMPUTER? THE KEYBOARD IS FULL OF CORN SYRUP!

I WANT MY TURN.

PARDON ME?

AT YOUR DESK. IT'S THE PERFECT EXCUSE TO GET NOTHING DONE.

OH NO YOU DON'T! I'VE GOT SENIORITY!

ET TU, TAMARA?

I JUST WANT YOU TO APPROVE MY SPRING STORYTIME SCHEDULE.

OH MY GOODNESS!

THEY'RE JUST BOOKS. LIBRARIES ARE FULL OF 'EM.

AUDIO BOOKS.

OH MY GOSH!

AND THIS IS OUR BRANCH MANAGER, WHO WILL CONTINUE YOUR INEXPLICABLY DELIGHTFUL TOUR.

OH MY JOY!

AND THIS IS TAMARA, OUR CHILDREN'S LIBRARIAN.

TAMARA, MEET THE ONLY LADY WHO CAN OUT-HAPPY YOU.

OH MY! PLEASED TO MEET YOU!

SHE'LL LOVE ANYTHING YOU SHOW HER.

HAVE YOU EVER FELT A FELT BOARD?

OH MY! TERRIFIC!

I'M AS DELIGHTED AT HER DELIGHT AS ANYONE, BUT I NEED TO GET SOME WORK DONE.

ALREADY DID MY SHIFT.

OH MY STARS!

OKAY MISS DELIGHTED-BY-EVERYTHING-SHE-SEES, THIS IS WHERE WE CAUGHT TWO TEENS IN THE THROES OF PASSION.

OH MY!

MEETING ROOM

THIS SPOT? BLOOD.

OH NO.

AND FINALLY, OUR TOP-SECRET STAIN REMOVAL LABORATORY...

NO, NO, YOU SNAPPED ME OUT OF IT.

I JUST TOLD HIM HIS MYSPACE "FRIENDS" AREN'T REALLY HIS FRIENDS.

I CAN'T GET THIS POSTER OUT OF ITS SLEEVE!

STAND BACK!

THAT HELPED ME HOW?

LIBRARY TIP#34: UNDERSTAND THE TECHNOLOGY

I THOUGHT IT WAS A TOUCH SCREEN.

IT'S NOT.

I THOUGHT I COULD DRAW ON IT.

YOU CAN'T.

ACTUALLY I COULD.

YOU USED A PERMANENT MARKER.

OOH, NICE SMILEY FACE!

NOT AGAIN.

THIS IS NANCY, THE READING ADVOCACY CHICKEN.

IT TOOK TENS OF THOUSANDS OF DOLLARS AND HUNDREDS OF HOURS, BUT A TEAM OF CONSULTANTS WAS ABLE TO IDENTIFY HER AS THE BEST WAY TO PROMOTE READING.

THAT'S RIDICU...

BOOK! BOOK! BOOK! BOOK!

MOM? SUDDENLY I THINK I'D LIKE TO FIND MYSELF A BOOK!

WHILE WE'RE LUCKY ENOUGH TO HAVE NANCY YOU WON'T BE DOING STORYTIMES.

BUT—

THEY'RE INEFFICIENT. YOU REQUIRE PREP TIME. ALL NANCY NEEDS IS CORN!

BOOK! BOOK! BOOK! BOOK!

THAT CHICKEN! I'D READ ANYTHING!

WILL NANCY HANDLE MY JOB TOO?

AFRAID NOT. NANCY JUST DOESN'T HAVE THE SAME EFFECT ON TEENS.

BOOK YOURSELF.

UNSHELVED

ON THE ROAD

When we started making this comic strip we never expected we'd end up being flown to the every corner of the country to speak at book, comic, and, especially, library conferences. But that's what we do. And when we're not speaking we're signing *Unshelved* books and selling *Unshelved* t-shirts, jackets, hats, bookbags, and, though I'll have to double-check this to be sure, thong underwear.

Well, it beats working.

Our friends can't figure it out. They ask "What do you *talk* about?" (ourselves, the comic strip, libraries, graphic novels, customer service) and "People *pay* you for that?" (yes) and "They *laughed*?" (yes) and "They gave you a *standing ovation*?" (occasionally).

And then there are the really big conferences, the ones where we get a booth. There's Book Expo America, there's Comic-Con International, but if you make a comic strip about a library the place to be is at the mother of all library conferences, the American Library Association (ALA) annual conference. In that exhibit hall, for four days, we are famous. It's a really short-term, niche, undeserved kind of fame, but we'll take it (especially Bill).

Conferences are such peculiar things that we started documenting our experiences in a set of *Unshelved* comic strips published only in the ALA conference newsletter (and reprinted in these books). We call them "Conference Tips", and what follows is one year's worth. The highlight was when ALA held its conference in our hometown of Seattle. Not only because we got to write what amounted to "Seattle *Unshelved*." But because we didn't need to fly anywhere.

If you want to see what the (totally unwarranted) fuss is about, check our website (www.unshelved.com). We're doubtless coming soon to a conference near you.

CONFERENCE TIP: USE YOUR SUPER-SENSES

CONFERENCE TIP: THROW SOFTBALLS

CONFERENCE TIP: AVOID WORK-RELATED METAPHORS

CONFERENCE TIP: THEY CALL THEM "CARGO PANTS" FOR A REASON

CONFERENCE TIP: PREPARE FOR SEATTLE

CONFERENCE TIP: ENJOY LOCAL ATTRACTIONS

CONFERENCE TIP: BE ORIGINAL WHEN MOCKING THE WEATHER

CONFERENCE TIP: JUST ASK FOR WHAT YOU WANT

CONFERENCE TIP: PAY EXTRA TO HAVE YOUR FRESH SALMON SENT TO YOU

UNSHELVED BOOK CLUB

When one makes a comic strip about a library one feels a certain obligation to write comic strips about books. But really, what are we going to do, make Michael Crichton jokes? Okay, we did actually do that once. But it doesn't scale very well. What we wanted to do was to recommend books, but our initial attempts felt a little flat. After all, it is a *comic strip*. It's supposed to be *funny*. How do you talk about books in a funny way without making fun of the book and/or its author? We traded ideas back and forth for literally years before we finally stumbled on the answer (which, as usually happens, was blindingly obvious in retrospect): it's not *books* that are funny, it's *people* that are funny. Get our *characters* talking about books and the humor will flow.

And so it has. Mind you, at the breakneck pace of one per week we aren't exactly competing with *The New York Review of Books*, but we're having fun recommending titles based on the exacting criteria of "we liked it." And the response has been nothing short of tremendous. Libraries, schools, and bookstores post our strips alongside the books in question, which then *fly off the shelves*. Anecdotally, anyway, we haven't seen any airborne literature ourselves.

The hardest part is that we feel a compulsion to read more broadly than we would if we were just feeding our own proclivities. Instead of mining our collective way through a favorite sci-fi/fantasy writer like termites through wood, we forage broadly across authors and genres. If one of us reads a great book the other one turns a blind eye and shoulders on bravely to the next title on the stack.

For Bill it's been an artistic challenge to, essentially, illustrate a book cover every week. We're starting to feature occasional guest strips from some of our cartoonist friends - this volume features the comic strip stylings of Mark Monlux, who in his feature *The Comic Critic* does for movies much what we do for books. And, as he will happily tell you, he did it first.

We've also started featuring graphic novels. Comics about comics - where will it all end? We hope you'll stick around and find out.

THE Unshelved® BOOK CLUB PRESENTS Ptolemy's Gate

BOOK 3 OF THE BARTIMAEUS TRILOGY

BY Jonathan Stroud

In *Ptolemy's Gate*, England's magicians rule by the power of demons they summon.

But their empire is crumbling.

The war in the Americas isn't going well.

And back at home, rebellion is in the air.

John Mandrake is a teenage prodigy who rose to the highest levels of power with the help of his witty demon Bartimaeus.

He's investigating a plot against the government when he finds Kitty, a smart young revolutionary he long thought dead.

She may hold the answers to all his (and England's) problems --

-- if they can live through an evening at the theatre!

Imagine - a world where demons can be controlled!

I wish.

BB

I've been reviewing your performance over the past year.

You don't exactly hit a lot of home runs.

The library can't afford home run hitters.

The Oakland A's manager, Billy Beane, had the same problem.

He needed to win games but he couldn't afford to pay for big name players.

Moneyball tells how he and his statistician re-defined talent and drafted players other teams wouldn't even consider hiring.

They focused on batters' on-base percentages and pitchers' abilities to get batters to ground out, not home runs and speed.

They had a winning season with the smallest payroll in the Major League.

David JUSTICE LEFT FIELD

Miguel TEJADA SHORT

Germaine DYE RIGHT FIELD

Athletics

CH THIR

What's your point?

That I have a very small strike zone.

And I deserve a raise.

Hey, I got to first base last night!

But you're not on a baseball team.

READ

BB

AMAZING GRACE

BY MEGAN SHULL

Fifteen-year-old Grace "Ace" Kincaid, tennis superstar, has had enough of dieticians and workouts and product endorsements.

She tells her mother she wants out.

She cancels her contracts, fires her manager, and says goodbye to her bodyguard.

Her "aunt" takes her to a remote Alaskan town where she can live until the media furor dies down.

While paparazzi try to hunt her down, Grace finds the love, life, and friendship she's been missing.

Oh! My! God!

Like anyone would choose to wear *flannel!*

BB

Today is my first day of retirement. I'm here for some reading matter!

That sounds wonderful.

Speaking of retirement, I was just reading *The Number* by Lee Eisenberg.

He says most people have an amount of money in mind — when they have that Number they can retire.

Unfortunately most people's Numbers are far too low.

They aren't thinking realistically about how they'll spend their retirement, and what it will cost.

They are overestimating rates of return and the stability of Social Security and pensions.

And they are underestimating expenses, medical costs, and unexpected crises.

They have the wrong Number.

So, what sort of reading matter would you like?

The "Help Wanted" section.

THE Unshelved® BOOK CLUB PRESENTS **MAROONED IN REALTIME** BY VERNOR VINGE

The end of the world has come and gone.

But there are survivors - time travelers from the past, brought to the distant future in time-stopping "bobbles".

With luck, they might just be able to restart the human race.

"bobbles"

YOU ARE HERE

2250 "SINGULARITY" (all humanity disappears)

DISTANT FUTURE

LAST HUMAN COLONY

Then Marta, co-founder of the colony, is murdered - left outside a bobble to die of old age.

Wil Brierson, the last detective on Earth, has to solve a Whodunnit with the highest stakes of all.

6'

5'

Did Marta's lover kill her out of jealousy?

Was it the Republic of New Mexico, the world's last democracy?

Or the family that wants to personally witness the end of the universe?

Or the Peace Authority, who used Bobbles to rule the world?

Or Della Lu, star pilot and Wil's investigative partner?

2'

Oh, and there's the little mystery of what happened to the rest of humanity.

And who bobbled Wil, tearing him away from his wife and children?

But first things first.

Rincewind is a very bad wizard. He got kicked out of wizard school and only knows one spell.

Now he's a reluctant tour guide for Twoflower, an insurance agent from the other side of Discworld who can't seem to understand that most of the "quaint attractions" are profoundly deadly.

My favorite character: the magic luggage that follows Twoflower everywhere.

It's the first book of a hysterical series that turns genre conventions on their heads.

Fantasy novels are supposed to be humorless epics!

No they aren't.

I rolled an 18. You're banished to a nether dimension.

No I'm not.

APATHY
AND OTHER SMALL VICTORIES

Shane drifts into New York City on a Greyhound.

He's drunk all the time.

To pay the rent, he sleeps with his landlord's wife every Tuesday.

His work-obsessed girlfriend nearly kills him in bed and then analyzes their nonexistent relationship.

He naps all day in the bathroom at work and throws away the documents he's supposed to be alphabetizing.

He's pretty sure he didn't kill her, and very sure that someone driving the General Lee is trying to kill him.

Now she's dead and he's a suspect.

His only friend is his dentist's deaf receptionist, who taught him to swear in sign language.

That book couldn't sound more offensive!

Did I mention his neighbor's questionable relationship with his guinea pig?

THE Unshelved® BOOK CLUB PRESENTS THE WRECKERS BY IAIN LAWRENCE

The *Isle of Skye* was in trouble.

A sudden storm forced them to seek safe harbor.

But the beacon on the cliffs led them to ruin on the rocks.

14-year-old John Spencer has to escape the men who want the ship's cargo -- and no witnesses to their crime!

Like when the sirens Pisinoe, Aglaope, and Thelxiepia tried to lure Odysseus to his death!

Now the Argonauts --

Quick, take this book before she starts reciting *The Iliad*.

I've got the perfect book for this situation!

It's full of practical advice on just such a topic.

Like how to spot a robot mimicking a person: Does it smell like a new soccer ball?

Doesn't apply.

The robot weapon of choice: lasers. So keep welder's goggles handy.

Maybe we can flee past the hardware store.

As far as karate: don't bother unless you can punch through metal.

Never crossed my mind.

Let's run for a body of water. The robot's heavy, it should sink.

This is Mallville. All we've got are parking lots.

This never would have happened in my day!

BB

Gregor and his sister fall through a grating in their New York City laundry room into an underground world.

Humans called "Underlanders" live there along with giant sentient cockroaches, bats, rats, and spiders.

Gregor's missing father is a prisoner of the rats

The Underlanders believe Gregor is the warrior told of in an ancient prophecy and aid him in his quest to free his father.

Cockroaches are their friends?

Of course. Every creature on Earth deserves our love and respect.

But they're fighting rats.

Filthy creatures! I wish they'd all die die *die*!

um, humanely and peacefully?

Nice try, Gandhi.

THE Unshelved® BOOK CLUB PRESENTS THE WARRIOR'S APPRENTICE
BY LOIS MCMASTER BUJOLD

A poison attack on his pregnant mother left Miles Vorkosigan stunted, his bones brittle as glass.

All he wanted was to be a Barrayaran soldier like his famous father.

But when he breaks his legs - again - he's kicked out of the military.

At seventeen Miles' life on Barrayar is over.

But never count Miles out.

The Warrior's Apprentice tells how this remarkable young man talks, fights, and bluffs his way into the life of his dreams.

On a trip to his mother's home planet, an act of kindness begins a cascade of events that will place Miles in command of an interstellar mercenary army.

Don't you have books with more attractive protagonists?

Miles Vorkosigan is one of the greatest characters in science fiction. He's brilliant, quick-witted, and charming!

Yeah, like I said, I can't really relate.

THE STUPIDEST ANGEL
a Heartwarming Tale of Christmas Terror
BY CHRISTOPHER MOORE

14-year-old Giannine is playing a total immersion video game called *Heir Apparent*.

She plays a sheepherder named heir to the throne. Her goal: survive three older brothers, the queen, puzzles, monsters, rebels, and 1000 other ways to die.

But there's a real problem: *Citizens to Protect Our Children*, who believe the world should be G-rated, have sabotaged the program.

If she doesn't beat the game she could die for real.

I don't get it.

World of Warcraft meets *Little Bo Peep*.

Thomas Stein just negotiated a multimillion-dollar fee for his client, the hottest starlet in Hollywood.

His name is all over the industry tabloids.

He's got the world on a string.

Then his boss introduces him to his newest client, the alien Joshua.

Tom's mission: get the American public to love Joshua's friendly race.

If only they weren't nauseatingly ugly and smelly...

It's an allegory for the homeless problem!

It is?

And I'll bet he comes up with the same solution I did:

Scented kitty litter in my pockets!

THE Unshelved® BOOK CLUB PRESENTS **THE GAME**
PENETRATING THE SECRET SOCIETY OF PICKUP ARTISTS
BY NEIL STRAUSS

Reporter Neil Strauss was just another shy loser, afraid to talk to women.

Then he was assigned to infiltrate the shadowy community of pickup artists.

Soon he learned tricks I've been using all my life.

Dress to stand out - the more outrageous, the better!

Start with a disparaging remark to throw her off balance.

Isolate your target, using wingmen to distract her friends.

Follow the rules of *The Game* and you too can make it with the sexy lady of your choice!

Should I buy her some ice cream?

No! Make her buy it herself!

Okay, Romeo, you're out of here.

THE GAME

NICK & NORAH'S
INFINITE PLAYLIST
BY RACHEL COHN AND DAVID LEVITHAN

Tris broke Nick's heart three weeks ago.

She was in the crowd at his queercore band's show.

Norah needed a ride home for her drunk girlfriend.

That's why he asked Norah to be his five minute girlfriend.

That's why she agreed to be Nick's 5 minute girlfriend.

He tried to give her and her friend a ride home in Jessie, his Yugo, but it wouldn't start.

That's also why she extended the deal.

So his bandmates threw Norahs' friend into their van and sent Nick and Norah on their way.

But then his car wouldn't start and her ex called her a Tin Woman and then his bandmates gave her cash for a night out with Nick (and her friend a ride home).

Nick and Norah aren't sure who each other are, but their mutual something is starting to matter.

And they've agreed to go watch nuns make out (it's better than a three-way with an alien).

I don't get it.

That's because it's for your daughter.

Then why are you telling **me** about it?

Because, as with most edgy well-written teen novels, if I told **her** about it you could have me fired.

CAMERA OBSC

WOLF BROTHER
BY MICHELLE PAVER

A bear, possessed by a demon, attacked Torak and his Fa.

As Torak's father lay dying, he made Torak swear to find the Mountain of the World Spirit before the bear becomes invincible.

He has his father's knife, his sleeping sack, an ax, a medicine pouch, and the knowledge that his father gave him: *his guide will find him.*

He must survive the wilderness alone, find the mountain, and destroy the bear to save the Forest.

But the bear won't be the only thing hunting Torak.

Is it very violent?

No.

Spiritual?

Definitely.

I want him to have good values and respect nature.

It'll be perfect.

One character has to be really into macramé.

Don't push it.

THE THIEF

BY MEGAN WHALEN TURNER

THE Unshelved® BOOK CLUB PRESENTS THE CITY OF EMBER
BY JEANNE DuPRAU

ReadyMade

HOW TO MAKE (ALMOST) EVERYTHING: A DO-IT-YOURSELF PRIMER

SHOSHANA BERGER, TEXT • GRACE HAWTHORNE, PROJECTS

ReadyMade tought me to see old materials in a new context.

(There's even a list of alternative uses for the book)

It's got essays on the science of paper, plastic, wood, metal, glass, and fabric.

I made CD racks out of old FedEx containers

Plus "related" topics like how to avoid *plastic* surgery.

a (noisy) lounge chair from empty plastic bottles.

But the projects were the best part.

and picture frames from old hardcovers

So you want me to make stuff out of garbage.

I want to help you save the earth while you save money!

I don't know.

I made this for you. It's a soda can shoji screen. But I added some custom pixelated art.

Yes, your aluminum sculpture goes beautifully with your dirty laundry.

I've recontextualized my laundry. It's a chair until Wednesday.

Alanna: The First Adventure

BY TAMORA PIERCE

Alanna of Trebond wants to be a Knight of Tortall.

She became Alan and took her brother's place as a page in the palace of King Roald.

She will find magic in an ancient ruin, befriend the King of Thieves, and face the Nameless One in the Black City.

But first she needs to face the bully who has been brutalizing her.

And she needs to do it alone.

Ralon of Malven has beggers and thieves for ancestors. He's the son of a lizard and a demon. He has all the honor of a weasel.

Please stop doing that!

I'd listen to your sister if I were you.

Why, because of your stupid book?

No, because in a few years she's going to stop asking so politely.

THE ROGUE'S GAME
BY MILTON T. BURTON

VEGAN WITH A VENGEANCE
OVER 150 DELICIOUS, CHEAP, ANIMAL-FREE RECIPES THAT ROCK
BY ISA CHANDRA MOSKOWITZ

I'm through apologizing for vegan food.

And I owe it all to this book.

It's a vegan book without a salad recipe.

(And it's worth the price of the book to learn how to cut a butternut squash.)

It includes mainstream foods that have been veganized. It's made me fearless in the kitchen.

So stop looking like someone who lost a bet.

I'll just sit here waiting patiently for my dry, tasteless veggie burger to appear.

Lemon corn waffles with blueberry sauce

Faustess cupcakes

Sweet potato fries

Baked cajun french fries

No-bake black bottom peanut butter silk pie

But I'm trying to get him to eat nutritiously!

"Vegan" doesn't mean "healthy".

I figure he'll kill himself eating junk food anyway

At least tonight nothing else had to die.

The Unshelved® BOOK CLUB PRESENTS

WHAT WE BELIEVE BUT CANNOT PROVE
TODAY'S LEADING THINKERS ON SCIENCE IN THE AGE OF UNCERTAINTY
EDITED BY JOHN BROCKMAN

"WHAT DO YOU BELIEVE IS TRUE, EVEN THOUGH YOU CANNOT PROVE IT?"

NO PART OF MY CONSCIOUSNESS WILL SURVIVE MY DEATH.

IAN McEWAN
AUTHOR, ENDURING LOVE, AMSTERDAM, ATONEMENT

WE'RE IN FOR CLIMATIC MAYHEM.

BRUCE STERLING
NOVELIST, JOURNALIST AND FUTURIST

TODAY'S CHILDREN ARE UNINTENDED VICTIMS OF ECONOMIC AND TECHNOLOGICAL PROGRESS.

DANIEL GOLEMAN
AUTHOR, EMOTIONAL INTELLIGENCE

LIFE IS COMMON THROUGHOUT THE UNIVERSE AND WE WILL FIND ANOTHER EARTHLIKE PLANET WITHIN THE DECADE.

STEPHEN PETRANEK
EDITOR-IN-CHIEF DISCOVER MAGAZINE

DEWEY DECIMAL PWNS LIBRARY OF CONGRESS.

ELSIE
CATALOGER

SEXUAL ORIENTATION IS NOT A CHOICE.

MEL
BRANCH MANAGER

MY BIRTH PARENTS LOVE ME VERY MUCH.

DOREEN
PRESCHOOLER

I'M GOING TO BE RICH.

AND FAMOUS.

AND TALL.

MERV
HIGH SCHOOLER

TASTES GREAT.

NO, LESS FILLING.

BUDDY THE BOOK BEAVER
LIBRARY PAGE

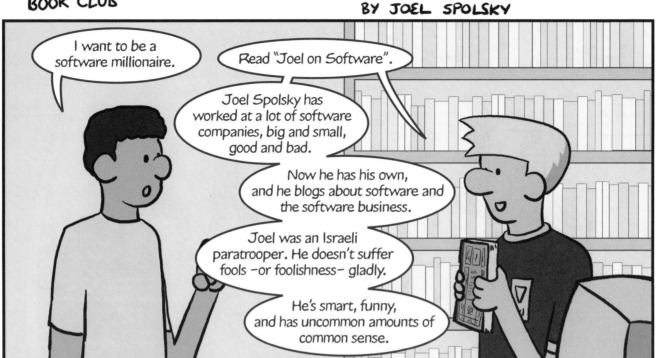

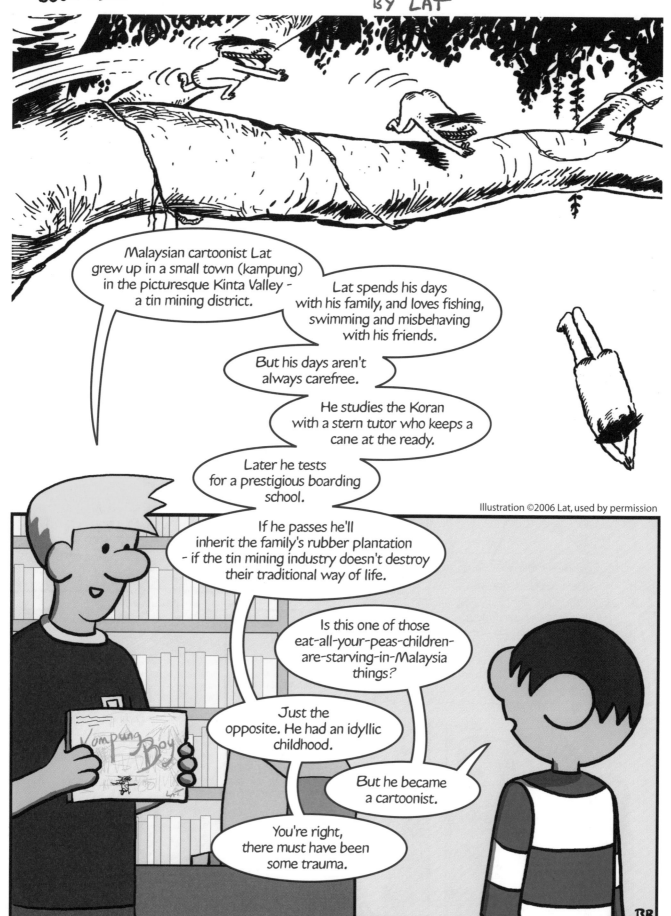

THE **Unshelved**® BOOK CLUB PRESENTS

KAMPUNG BOY
BY LAT

Malaysian cartoonist Lat grew up in a small town (kampung) in the picturesque Kinta Valley - a tin mining district.

Lat spends his days with his family, and loves fishing, swimming and misbehaving with his friends.

But his days aren't always carefree.

He studies the Koran with a stern tutor who keeps a cane at the ready.

Later he tests for a prestigious boarding school.

Illustration ©2006 Lat, used by permission

If he passes he'll inherit the family's rubber plantation - if the tin mining industry doesn't destroy their traditional way of life.

Is this one of those eat-all-your-peas-children-are-starving-in-Malaysia things?

Just the opposite. He had an idyllic childhood.

But he became a cartoonist.

You're right, there must have been some trauma.

THE **Unshelved**® PRESENTS
BOOK CLUB

THE FORESHADOWING
BY MARCUS SEDGWICK

17-year-old Sasha's oldest brother, Edward, has gone to France to do his duty on the frontlines.

Their brother Tom tried to attend medical school, but society and their father brand him a coward – he finally gives in and joins the infantry.

She volunteers as a nurse at her father's hospital, but her gift makes that difficult:

All her life she's been able to foresee the deaths of others.

Contact with wounded soldiers makes her visions difficult to ignore.

And then she foresees Tom's death and sets off to stop it.

She sees dead people? What is this, *The Sixth Sense* meets *A Farewell to Arms?*

Not at all. It's a detailed portrait of the British home front and the French battlefields during World War I.

Dang.

Shyamalan might direct the movie.

Wow!

Really?

No.

Will you say anything to put a book in someone's hands?

Yes.

RATS

BY PAUL ZINDEL

THE HUSTLER
BY WALTER TEVIS

When Fast Eddie Felson walked into Bennington's to play Minnesota Fats he was the best pool hustler in the country.

When he walked out he was a broken man.

And he hadn't hit bottom yet.

Before he can take on Minnesota Fats again he'll need to pick up a girl, find someone to stake him, and figure out what it takes to be a winner.

That's because he didn't have laser targeting.

That's what I like about you, your enduring respect for tradition.

You are a very sincere person. You take things at face value. I respect that.

But our world is steeped in irony. You need to understand it.

I understand irony.

For instance...?

Mrs. Silver has silver hair.

Coincidence.

That t-shirt was probably made in a sweatshop.

Hypocrisy.

FAIR LABOR

What do William Shakespeare, O. Henry, Bill Murray, and Stephen Colbert have in common?

Sometimes I don't get their jokes.

Precisely.

Guess what credit card companies call cardholders who pay their bills in full every month?

"Good customers"?

"Deadbeats".

STAFF

Why do we need irony? Why can't everyone be like me?

One of the questions this book attempts to answer.

The Big Book of Irony?

But it's really quite small!

BB

THE UNSHELVED BOOK CLUB PRESENTS **WHATCHA MEAN, WHAT'S A ZINE?**
THE ART OF MAKING ZINES AND MINI-COMICS
BY MARK TODD & ESTHER PEARL WATSON

Practical!

Zines were blogs before blogs were blogs. They're smaller than small press but can lead to careers.

when is a blog not a blog?

They're small, 100% personal "magazines" made with photocopiers and mimeograph machines or by hand on paper or matchbooks or whatever is on hand.

Inspirational

THEIR CONTENT IS INSPIRED AND HANDCRAFTED — COLLAGE, COMICS, PHOTOS, DRAWINGS, ESSAYS, LETTERS, FICTION, REVIEWS — ANYTHING!

CUT AND PASTE

This book includes their history (with pages and pages by pioneers) plus lots of advice on how to make (copier tricks, printing, silkscreen, assembling, binding) your own + info on how to get folks to read and even pay for yours!

Testimonial!

YOU KNOW, A GOOD DESKTOP PUBLISHING PROGRAM WOULD CLEAN THIS RIGHT UP!

LET ME START AGAIN

© 2007 Overdue Media LLC unshelved.com
Unshelved by Bill Barnes + Gene Ambaum